NATIONAL GEOGRAPHIC
Ladders
It's a Home Run!

GENRE Song

Read to find out about the story told in this baseball song.

Take Me Out to the BALL GAME

words by Jack Norworth
music by Albert Von Tilzer

In many ballparks, it's a **tradition** to sing "Take Me Out to the Ball Game" during the seventh-inning stretch. Most fans can sing along with the **refrain,** but did you know there are two **verses,** too? Together with the refrain, the verses tell a story about Katie Casey, a girl who is a big fan of America's **national pastime,** baseball.

REFRAIN

Take me out to the ball game,
Take me out with the crowd.
Buy me some peanuts and Cracker Jack,
I don't care if I never get back,
Let me root, root, root for the home team,
If they don't win it's a shame.
For it's one, two, three strikes, you're out,
At the old ball game.

root cheer
sou a small amount of money
beau boyfriend

VERSE 1

Katie Casey was baseball mad.
Had the fever and had it bad;
Just to root for the hometown crew,
Ev'ry sou Katie blew.
On a Saturday, her young beau
Called to see if she'd like to go,
To see a show but Miss Kate said,
"No, I'll tell you what you can do."

VERSE 2

Katie Casey saw all the games,
Knew the players by their first names;
Told the umpire he was wrong,
All along good and strong.
When the score was just two to two,
Katie Casey knew what to do,
Just to cheer up the boys she knew,
She made the gang sing this song:

Check In How would you describe Katie Casey?

GENRE History Article **Read to find out** about baseball history and traditions.

The Old Ball Game

by Michael Bilski

BASEBALL IS BORN

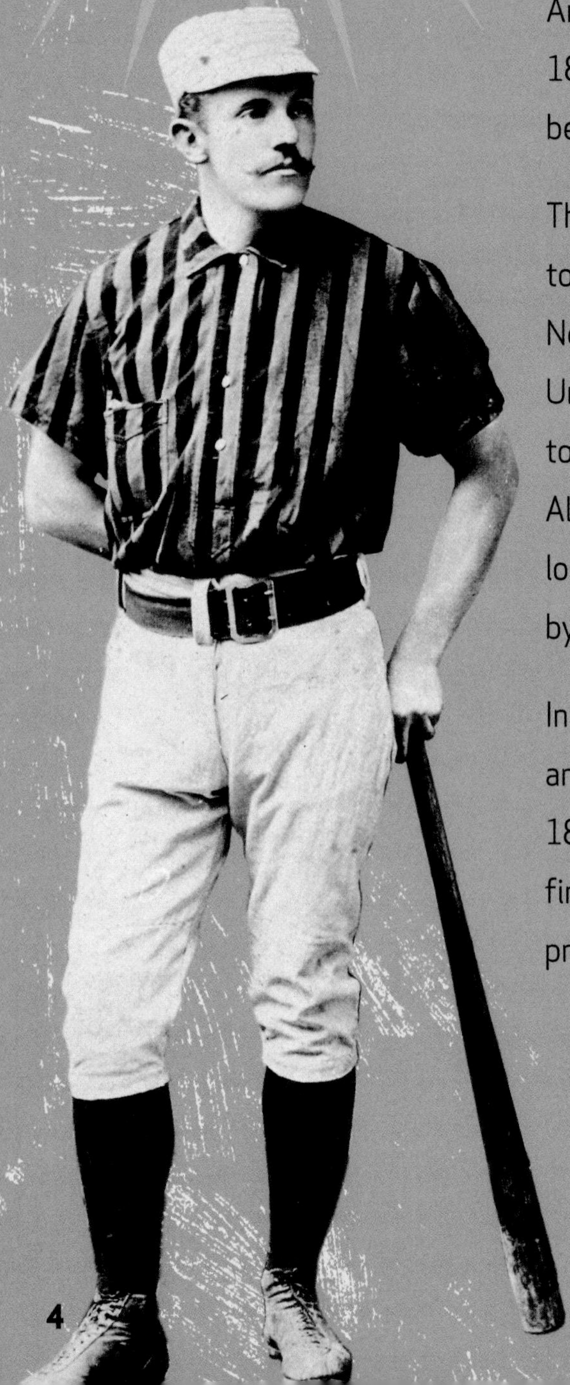

Americans have enjoyed baseball since the early 1800s. Over time, it grew so popular that it became known as America's **national pastime.**

The basic rules of baseball as we know them today were set by Alexander Cartwright and the New York Knickerbocker Base Ball Club in 1845. Until then, players could hit a runner with the ball to make an out. Ouch! This led to many fights. Although the Knickerbockers made the rules, they lost the first game they played with the new rules by a score of 23 to 1!

In the early days of baseball, teams played for fun and were not paid. Over time that changed, and in 1869 the Cincinnati Red Stockings became the first professional team to pay all its players. Soon, professional leagues arose.

Elysian Fields in Hoboken, New Jersey

1846

The Knickerbockers play the first baseball game using the new rules in Hoboken, New Jersey.

1866

The first women's baseball team is started at Vassar College.

1845

Alexander Cartwright and the Knickerbockers list the rules of baseball.

Alexander Cartwright

1869

The Cincinnati Red Stockings, the first all-professional team, play their first game.

The Cincinnati Red Stockings, 1869

1876

The National League is formed.

William Hulbert, founder of the National League

IT'S IN THE CARDS

As baseball grew, so did baseball **traditions.** The tradition of collecting cards began in the 1860s. In the 1870s, companies produced baseball cards to help sell their products. Decades later one of the most successful card makers, the Topps Chewing Gum Company, sold packs of gum with baseball cards inside.

As in the past, most fans today collect baseball cards for the fun of it. Some people, though, collect baseball cards for their value. Because it was rare, in fine condition, and showed future Hall of Fame player Honus Wagner, a 1909 card sold for $2,800,000 in 2007. Hold on to those baseball cards!

Baseball cards, late 1800s

MOSES FLEETWOOD WALKER

In 1884, Moses Fleetwood Walker became the first African American player to play baseball in a major league. He played for the Toledo Blue Stockings in the American Association, which was considered a major league at that time. It would be a long time before another African American would follow in Walker's footsteps.

1884

Moses Fleetwood Walker becomes the first African American player in the major leagues.

1887

Goodwin and Company makes the first widely distributed set of baseball cards.

1900

The American League is formed.

1903 World Series, Boston

1903

The first World Series is played. The Boston Americans defeat the Pittsburgh Pirates.

1907

Alta Weiss becomes the first professional woman baseball player.

Alta Weiss

1908

"Take Me Out to the Ball Game" is written.

1909

The famous Honus Wagner baseball card is printed.

BASEBALL CATCHES ON

The publication of "Take Me Out to the Ball Game" in 1908 was a sign that baseball had caught on with the public. In 1908, who would have guessed we would still be singing the song more than one hundred years later? Fans continue the tradition of singing "Take Me Out to the Ball Game" at many ballparks during the seventh-inning stretch. Singing along unites the fans, supports the home team, and adds to the fun of the game.

THE CEREMONIAL FIRST PITCH

In 1910, President Taft began a baseball tradition. He threw the ball onto the field at the first game of the new season in Washington, D.C. This began a tradition of presidents, other elected officials, and celebrities throwing what is known as the "ceremonial first pitch." Since 1910, all presidents except for Jimmy Carter have participated in this **ceremony.** Although Carter may have been too busy for baseball while president, he attended many Atlanta Braves games after leaving office.

President Taft on opening day, 1910

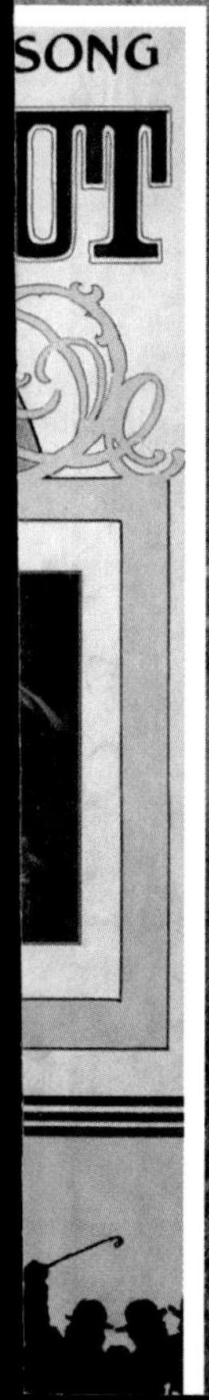

1910
President Taft throws the ceremonial first pitch on opening day.

1916
The Cleveland Indians become the first major league team with numbers on uniforms.

1917
The United States enters World War I.

1918
The "Star-Spangled Banner" is sung at a baseball game.

1919
Scandal! Reports say eight Chicago White Sox players take bribes and lose the World Series on purpose.

THE BATTLE BEYOND THE BALLPARK

In April of 1917, the United States entered World War I. Many young Americans, including baseball players, joined the military. As the war continued, a new musical tradition arose. At the 1918 World Series, a military band played "The Star-Spangled Banner" during the seventh-inning stretch to honor the servicemen who were at the game. After that, the song was played at every World Series game and every season opener. This tradition changed during World World II, when "The Star-Spangled Banner" was played before every game instead. That tradition continues to this day.

Players stand at attention for "The Star-Spangled Banner."

National League All-Star Team, 1933

LOOK AT ALL THE STARS!

One of baseball's annual traditions is the Major League All-Star Game. It is nicknamed the "Midsummer Classic" because it is played in July, about halfway into the baseball season. The first All-Star Game was played in July 1933 at Comiskey Park in Chicago. Baseball managers and fans chose stars from the American and National Leagues to play. Since then it has been a tradition for fans to vote for their favorite players for each year's game. All-Star Game voting strengthens the bond between players and fans, and lets the fans see the stars of the game gather on the same field.

1921

A baseball game is broadcast on radio for the first time.

1931

The Baseball Writers' Association begins a tradition. It names a "most valuable player" for each league.

1933

The first Major League All-Star Game is played.

1935
In Cincinnati, the first night game takes place.

1939
The National Baseball Hall of Fame and Museum opens.

1941
The United States enters World War II.

The girls' league in action

A HALL FOR BALL

The National Baseball Hall of Fame and Museum opened in 1939 in Cooperstown, New York. Every year, players are elected and **inducted** into the Hall. The candidates must have played within the last 20 years, have been retired for 5 years, and have played in the major leagues for at least 10 years. Candidates who receive at least 75 percent of the votes are inducted in a ceremony each summer. Only the best make it through the selection process. At the induction ceremony, each new member gives a speech and is honored with a plaque. Broadcasters, umpires, managers, and others important to baseball are elected in a separate process.

The National Baseball Hall of Fame and Museum

LET'S GO, LADIES!

From the beginning, professional baseball was a man's sport. During World War II, however, many baseball players joined the military and were not available to play. Baseball team owners had a problem: they didn't have enough male players to draw crowds. The solution? In 1943, the All-American Girls Professional Baseball League was formed. It started with just four teams, but had as many as ten teams during one season. The women drew crowds of as many as 10,000 people per game and more than 900,000 during their best season. The league even had its own victory song. Although the league disbanded in 1954, the players were pioneers for the girls and women playing today.

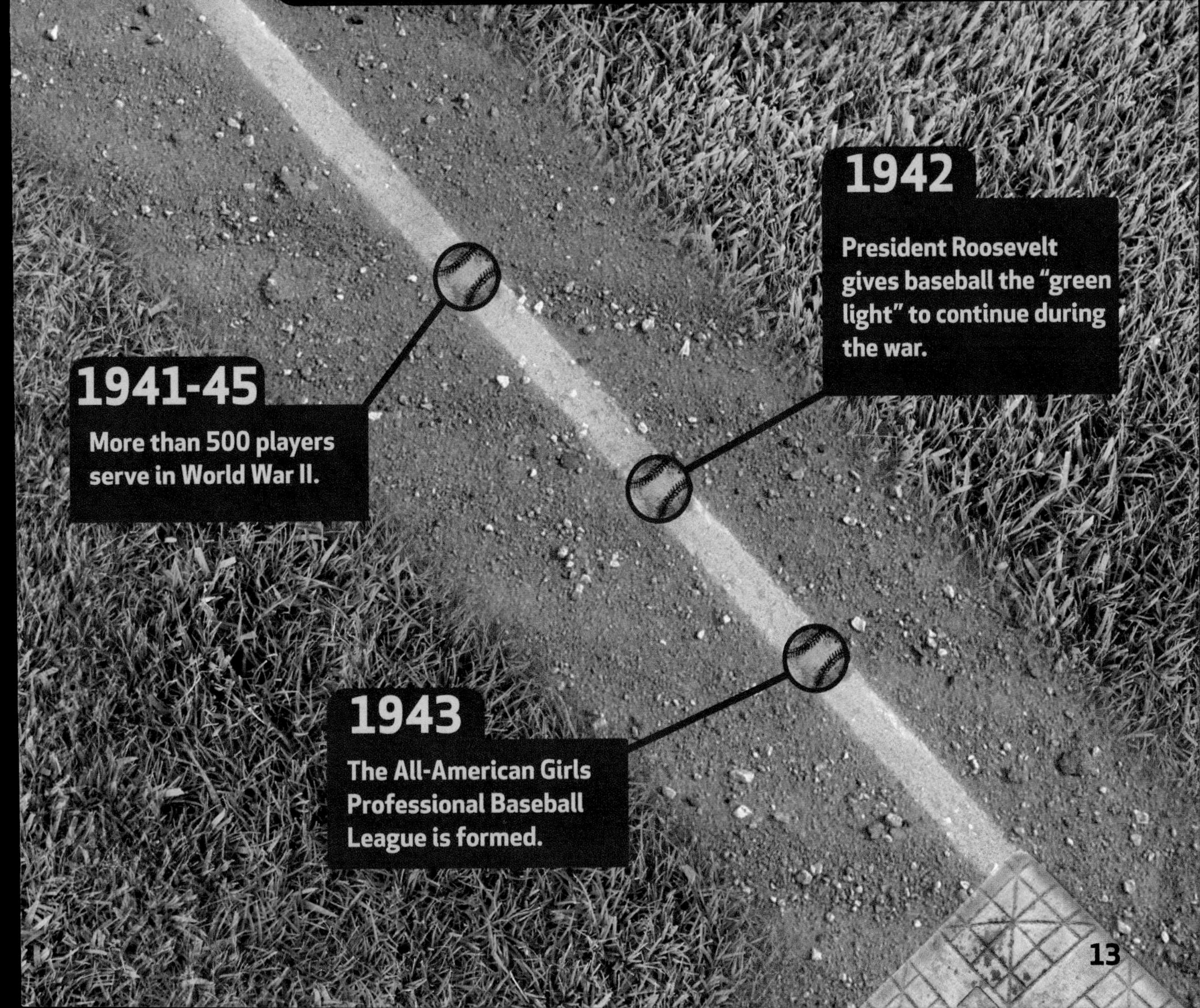

1947

Jackie Robinson becomes the first African American player in the major leagues since 1884.

ROGER MARIS

In 1961, Roger Maris hit his 61st home run, but fans weren't happy. Why? Because Maris had broken Babe Ruth's record of 60 home runs in a single season, set in 1927. Ruth was a legendary player, and fans didn't want Maris to topple his record. Some claimed that Maris didn't break it, since Ruth's record was set in a 154-game season, and Maris's in a 162-game season. The 61 home runs were just part of his amazing 1961 season. Maris was also voted the American League's Most Valuable Player and helped the Yankees win the World Series. What a season!

1947

The World Series is broadcast on TV for the first time.

Joe DiMaggio

LONG STREAKS

Fans are excited by record-setting long streaks. Joe DiMaggio had hits in 56 games in a row in 1941! Pete Rose's 44-game hitting streak in 1978 is the closest since then. Lou Gehrig played 2,130 games in a row for the New York Yankees, earning him a record that lasted for 56 years when Cal Ripken, Jr. of the Boston Orioles broke it in 1995. Ripken played in every game between May 30, 1982 and September 20, 1998. That's 2,632 games!

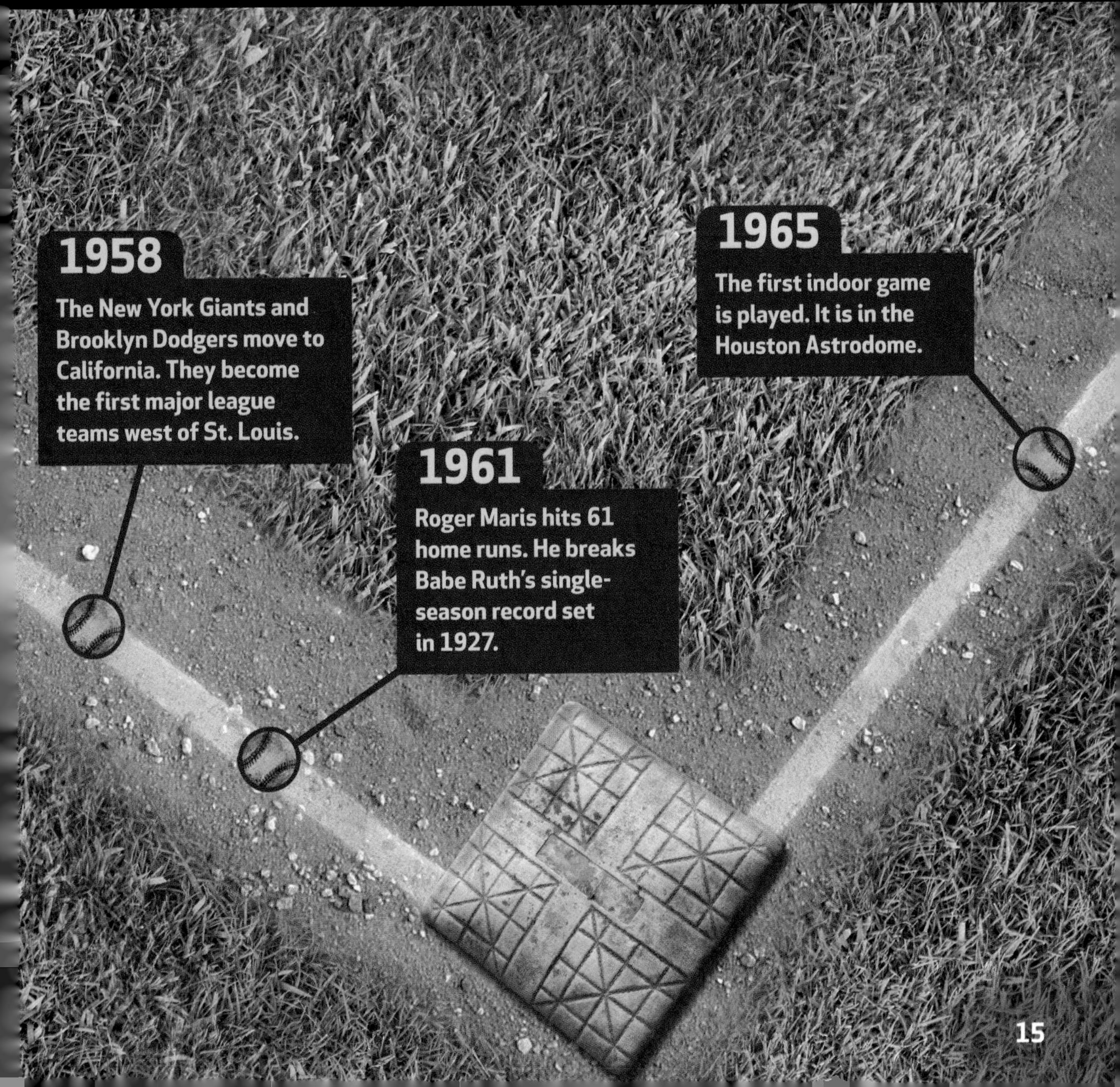

CELEBRATING A HERO

On April 15, 1947, Jackie Robinson of the Brooklyn Dodgers broke the color barrier. He became the first African American player in a major league since 1884. A new tradition began in 2004. That's when Major League Baseball began to celebrate Jackie Robinson Day. At each ballpark on April 15, every player, manager, coach, and umpire wears the number 42. That was Jackie's number. On all other days, that number is retired, so no one is allowed to wear it.

1972

Roberto Clemente dies in a plane crash.

1973

The American League begins to use the designated hitter rule.

ROBERTO CLEMENTE

From 1955 to 1972, the Pittsburgh Pirates had a great outfielder, Roberto Clemente. He was known for his skill in the game, as well as for his work to help people in need. In fact, Clemente died in a plane crash while taking supplies to earthquake survivors in Nicaragua in 1972. He was inducted into the Hall of Fame the next year, despite the rule a player could not be inducted until five years after the end of his baseball career. This rule was changed for Clemente because of the great things he did both on and off the field. Clemente was also the first Latin American player to be inducted.

1974

Hank Aaron breaks Babe Ruth's career home run record.

1997

Jackie Robinson's number 42 is retired.

2000

The Major League Baseball season opens in Japan for the first time.

2004

Jackie Robinson Day is celebrated for the first time.

WHAT'S NEXT?

Imagine what baseball might have been like in the 1840s, and then picture baseball today. So much has changed! Rules have been established. Professional leagues have grown, and players have become stars. Traditions have developed to celebrate important events. Records have been made and broken. Players from different backgrounds have become part of the game. Now imagine the future. What's next for baseball?

Check In Who has played an important role in the history of baseball? How?

GENRE Sports Article

Read to find out about other countries with professional baseball teams.

BASEBALL AROUND THE WORLD

by Michael Bilski

Although baseball started in the U.S. and became a **national pastime,** it soon spread to other countries, especially in Latin America and Asia. Whatever you call it—*béisbol, besuboru, or baseball*—it's an international sport with great players around the world.

National Baseball Hall of Fame and Museum Cooperstown, New York

Famous Players

Players come from many countries to play on major league teams in the U.S., and some of the best are honored in the Baseball Hall of Fame and Museum in Cooperstown, New York. The Hall has nine players (shown below) from other parts of the world. In the future, we're sure to see Hall of Famers from many more countries.

Halls of Fame

The U.S. isn't the only country with a national center to honor baseball. Other countries have halls of fame, too.

- The Japanese Baseball Hall of Fame and Museum opened in 1959. Trophies from the World Baseball Classic are proudly displayed there.
- The *Salón de la Fama y Museo del Béisbol Venezolano* opened in 1953 in Valencia, Venezuela. It's located in a building that is shaped like a baseball diamond.
- Cuba is home to the *Salón de la Fama del Béisbol Cubano*, which opened in 1939.
- The Korean Baseball Hall of Fame opened on Jeju Island in 1995. It has a library with 2,000 books and 800 films related to baseball.

THE WORLD BASEBALL CLASSIC

The World Baseball Classic (WBC) is an international competition that was held in 2006 and 2009. It will be held again in 2013, and 16 of the countries below will compete. In order to compete, teams must **qualify,** or do well in pre-WBC competition. Teams from the countries in red have competed successfully in the WBC before, so they already qualify. Teams from the countries in orange must qualify to compete.

1. AUSTRALIA
2. CHINA
3. CUBA
4. DOMINICAN REPUBLIC
5. ITALY
6. JAPAN
7. MEXICO
8. NETHERLANDS
9. PUERTO RICO
10. SOUTH KOREA
11. UNITED STATES
12. VENEZUELA
13. CANADA
14. CHINESE TAIPEI (TAIWAN)
15. PANAMA
16. SOUTH AFRICA
17. BRAZIL
18. COLOMBIA
19. CZECH REPUBLIC
20. FRANCE
21. GERMANY
22. GREAT BRITAIN
23. ISRAEL
24. NEW ZEALAND
25. NICARAGUA
26. SPAIN
27. PHILIPPINES
28. THAILAND

The World Baseball Classic

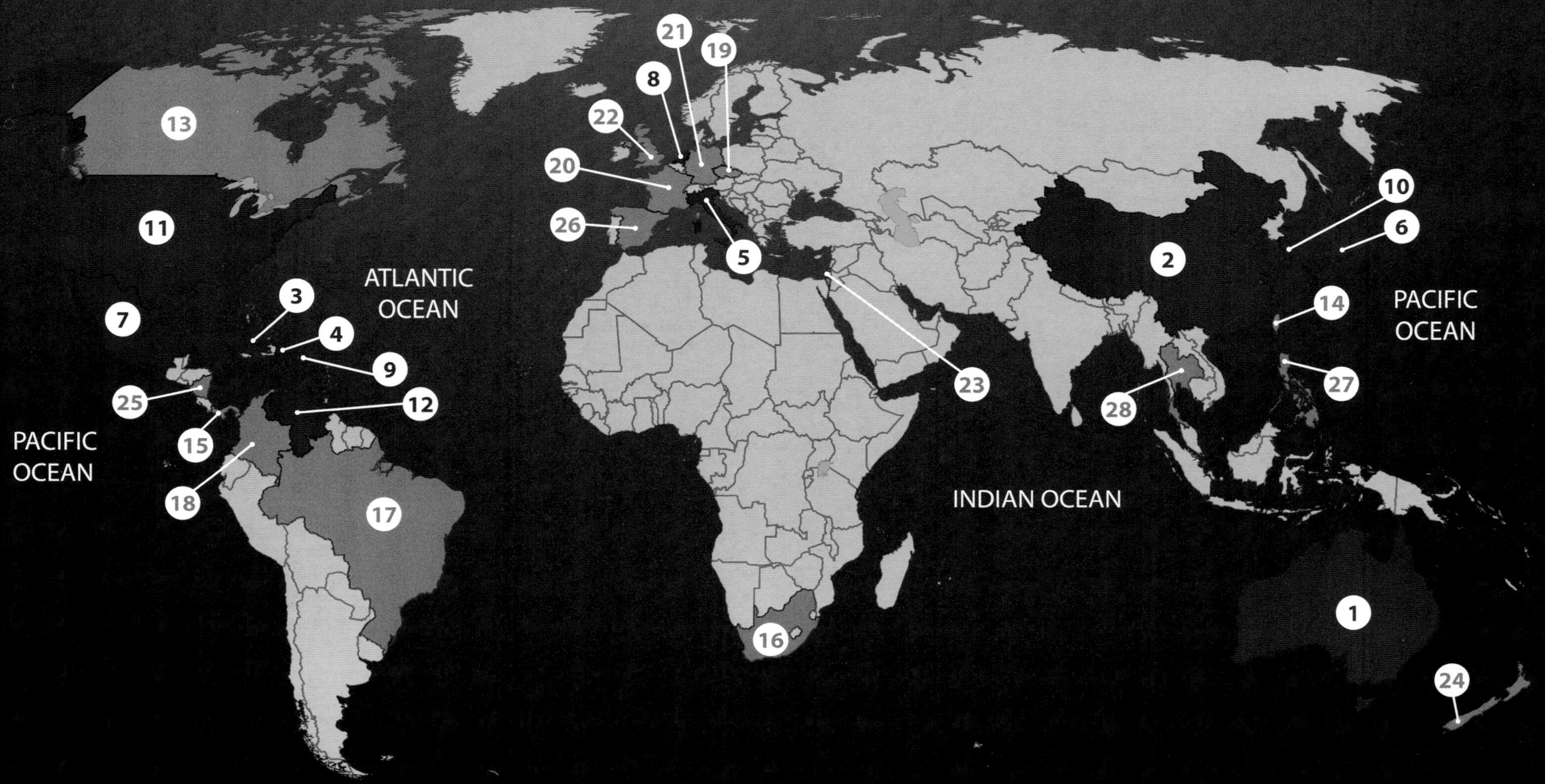

A World Tour

Let's take a closer look at a few countries in different parts of the world where professional baseball is played. The basic rules of the game are the same, but baseball **traditions** are influenced by the unique history and culture of each country.

ASIA

Japan

besuboru = *baseball* in Japanese

The Japanese have been playing baseball since the 1870s, when an American professor in Tokyo introduced the game. Since then, baseball has become Japan's most popular team sport, and fans there are every bit as enthusiastic as fans in the U.S. Throughout the game, they take part in organized cheers accompanied by cheerleaders dancing on the field. It's a tradition in some ballparks to release balloons during the seventh-inning stretch.

Japan won first place in both the 2006 and 2009 World Baseball Classic.

SOUTH AMERICA

Venezuela

béisbol = *baseball* in Spanish

Students returning home from colleges in the U.S. introduced baseball to Venezuela in the late 1800s. Although soccer is the most popular sport in most of Latin America, in Venezuela baseball dominates and fans flock to games. In the U.S. it may be a tradition to eat hot dogs at a ball game, but fans in Venezuela are likely to eat *arepas*, a type of cornbread with fillings such as ham and cheese.

Venezuela captured third place in the 2009 World Baseball Classic.

THE CARIBBEAN

Dominican Republic

béisbol = *baseball* in Spanish

Americans taught baseball to Cubans in the 1860s, and later the Cubans taught it to the Dominicans. Now baseball is the national sport of the Dominican Republic, and more major league players in the U.S. come from the DR than from any other foreign country. Fans there are enthusiastic, and many attend games with painted faces, flags, and noisemakers. If they get hungry, they can buy rice with beans at the ballpark.

In the 2006 World Baseball Classic, the Dominican Republic won fifth place.

EUROPE

Netherlands

honkbal = *baseball* in Dutch

In 1911, a Dutchman visited the U.S. and brought home a souvenir: the game of baseball! In Europe today, no country likes baseball more than the Netherlands. Despite baseball's popularity, though, soccer has more fans. In fact, one reason for baseball's appeal is that it fills the gap after the soccer season ends in the spring and before it resumes in the fall.

The Netherlands came in seventh place in the 2009 World Baseball Classic.

Check In Outside of the U.S., where is baseball the most popular?

Discuss Events and Time Lines

1. In what order is the information organized in "The Old Ball Game"? Why do you think it is organized in this way?

2. Choose an event in baseball that interests you. Explain what happened.

3. Choose a tradition in baseball. How do you think it helps players or fans?

4. In which baseball tradition would you most like to participate? Why?